Original title:
The Tropics Await

Copyright © 2025 Creative Arts Management OÜ
All rights reserved.

Author: Colin Leclair
ISBN HARDBACK: 978-1-80581-514-3
ISBN PAPERBACK: 978-1-80581-041-4
ISBN EBOOK: 978-1-80581-514-3

Fragrance of the Night Bloom

In the jungle, the monkeys swing,
Chasing dreams and banana bling.
Coconut cocktails, oh what a treat,
While parrots dance to a tropical beat.

Lizards in sunglasses, lounging around,
Cadillac crabs strutting on the ground.
Fireflies buzz, like a disco light,
While frogs serenade the stars at night.

Tiki torches flicker, the party ignites,
As palm trees sway in their funky heights.
A toucan tries to tell a joke,
But ends up tangled in a leaf of smoke.

So let's raise a glass, to the night so bright,
With laughter echoing 'til morning light.
The wild awaits, so don't be late,
In this colorful choo-choo of fate.

Symphony of the Aquatic Realm

Underwater giggles, a playful scene,
Where fish wear hats and the turtles preen.
Dolphins duet, with a splashy flair,
While seaweed sways in a dance fair.

Starfish clapping in a coral show,
An octopus juggles, putting on a glow.
Bubbles rise high, like balloons in the air,
As seahorses prance without a care.

Crabs play tag, with a sidestepping twist,
Their little claws clapping, not one is missed.
A splash from the whale, like a giant cheer,
"Join the party, folks, we're all right here!"

So dive into laughter, swim freely and roam,
In this aquatic wonder, we all find a home.
With giggles and bubbles, we serenade,
And ride the waves of this summer parade.

Parables of the Island Breeze

A seagull stole my sandwich, oh dear,
It squawked at me with raucous cheer.
I waved my arms and did a dance,
But it just laughed, took one last glance.

The palm trees swayed, they watched me plead,
The breeze now swirling, mocking my need.
A flip-flop flew, the sun did grin,
And laughter echoed on the island's skin.

Tranquil Footsteps on Ancient Paths

I tripped on roots like lively snakes,
Nature giggled as my balance breaks.
Old stones whispered tales of the past,
While I made friends with all things cast.

The path was crooked, like my own style,
Each step brought joy, and a little wile.
I sang to crabs, they waved their claws,
The forest chuckled, just because.

Dreams of Lush Shores

In my dreams, I surfed on bread,
A butter wave, I might be dead!
Seashells laughed, what a sight,
As jellyfish joined for a dance at night.

The sun was hot, my hat flew away,
A sunburned lobster did display.
I chased my thoughts, they ran so free,
In this silly dance by the wide sea.

Garden of Radiant Delights

In a garden where the fruits take flight,
Strawberries giggle in pure delight.
The cucumbers dance, oh, what a scene,
With tomatoes spinning, looking so keen.

I tried to hug a banana tree,
But it slipped away, just like a flea.
Carrots are grinning, peas in a row,
Join the banquet, come on, let's go!

Sweet Relief of the Evening Calm

As day fades out and stars come in,
I chase my cat who dreams of fish.
The sun's retreat is like a sin,
For now it's time to make a wish.

The air is thick with tales of glee,
My lemonade is wildly spun.
A hammock swings, no time for spree,
I nap and dream of jokes to run.

Trance of the Mellow Breeze

In sunsets where the palm trees twist,
I lose my hat upon a ride.
The breeze gives chase, it can't resist,
It flirts with laughter, docks with pride.

Each gust comes in with funny flair,
And tickles noses, makes them sneeze.
I swear the clouds begin to stare,
As I evade the buzzing bees.

Lullabies of the Island Spirits

The mermaids sing a crazy tune,
As I dive deep for seaweed snacks.
They giggle loud and blow up balloons,
While I catch waves and dodge the racks.

With coconuts as instruments,
I join their band and start to sway.
We dance around, the beach is tense,
While seagulls chuckle, fly away.

Colors of the Solstice

In skies adorned with shades so bright,
The sunset plays a game of tag.
I painted poppies, flew a kite,
And laughed at squirrels with a rag.

The rainbows sipped some fizzy drink,
While I slipped on a slimy slug.
With colors swirling, I can't think,
But giggles give my heart a tug.

Solace in the Shade

Underneath the swaying palm,
We find our peace, a soothing balm.
The sun's too bright, we wear a grin,
And sip on drinks with silly pins.

Lizards laugh, they play their games,
While we avoid those silly flames.
A hammock's weave, like a fine braid,
Inviting naps in the cool shade.

A parrot squawks, it tells a joke,
While I confuse a lizard for a bloke.
We munch on fruits that make us sing,
In shade we bask, let joy take wing.

So here's to shade, our favorite haunt,
Where laughter's loud, and we all flaunt.
In paradise, the goofballs play,
With every sip, we drift away.

Dances of the Ocean Blue

Waves roll in, they start to prance,
We stand on the shore, it's our first chance.
With little jumps and silly spins,
We dance like fish, our laughter wins.

The seaweed sways; it knows the beat,
We giggle loud, move our feet.
A crab joins in, trying to groove,
With sideways steps, it starts to prove.

Seagulls squawk, they cheer us on,
A fisherman shrugs, "This dance is wrong!"
But here beneath the sunny skies,
We craft our moves, with joyful sighs.

As shadows stretch, the sun dips low,
We spin and twirl, putting on a show.
With salty air, and hearts so free,
We dance on waves, our jubilee.

Enchantment Under the Mango Tree

Beneath the tree, where shadows meet,
Mangoes drop with a juicy greet.
With sticky hands, we laugh and tease,
While swatting flies, we feel the breeze.

A monkey swings, it knows our game,
As we munch fruit with naught but fame.
He steals a bite, then makes a face,
As juice runs down, he quickens pace.

The sun dips low, it casts a glow,
We giggle at the scene below.
With every bite, our worries fade,
In this sweet spot, we feel less frayed.

So let's make wishes, counting stars,
While fruit juice stains leave tiny scars.
Under this tree, our hearts are light,
In laughter's spell, we own the night.

Horizon's Embrace

At dawn we stretch, the sky's ablaze,
Caught in a trance, we lose our gaze.
The horizon calls, with colors bright,
"Chase the sun; it's pure delight!"

Flip-flops flop, and sand flies high,
As we hop and skip, oh my, oh my!
The ocean laughs, beckons us near,
With playful waves, we feel no fear.

A beach ball bounces, a seagull dives,
In this wild mix, our spirit thrives.
We chase the breeze, our joy in sight,
Floating dreams take off in flight.

So here's to mornings, golden and bold,
With silly hearts and tales retold.
In ocean's arms and sun's warm face,
We find our joy in horizon's embrace.

Dance of Shadows on the Sand

Footprints in the sun, they sway,
Dancing shadows lead the way,
A crab joins in, on sideways spree,
Chasing dreams, we laugh with glee.

The sun's a chef, it fries our toes,
While seagulls steal our chips, goodness knows,
We chase them down, all wild and free,
In this seaside comedy, just you and me.

Sandcastles crash like fashion trends,
While iguanas gossip like old friends,
Turtles munch on chips we throw,
Seems like beach life steals the show.

Laughter echoes in the breeze,
As we dodge the waves with perfect ease,
With every splash, the joy expands,
In this funny dance, all life's unplanned.

Emerald Dreams

Green is the color of this wild spree,
Palm fronds giggle in the sunny spree,
Monkeys swing with mischief in their eyes,
While parrots squawk as they get wise.

A lizard darts across my shoe,
I yell, 'Hey, what's your job?" Who knew?
With every step on this emerald ground,
The laughs of nature sing all around.

This jungle's a stage, watch me trip,
Over vines that seem to have a whip,
I wave hello to a flying frog,
He leaps away, 'Not my kind of bog!'

In emerald dreams, life's a mess,
We twirl and fall in tangled dress,
All around, the warmth, the cheer,
In this green-wrapped humor, life's crystal clear.

Whispering Palms

Palms whisper secrets, oh so sly,
As I dance and wave, they swing by,
Coconuts giggle, they drop with a thud,
A shower of laughter, a splash of good bud.

The wind plays matchmaker with hats,
Sending them sailing like playful cats,
My sunburnt nose tries to join the show,
"Hey, I'm fun too!" it cries in woe.

Eventful days in this swaying spree,
When a lazy iguana just stares at me,
"Are you my therapist? You've got style!"
I shrug back with a wink and a smile.

The sands are sticky, the juice is sweet,
With every trod, I feel the beat,
In moments of joy and soft palm sways,
We dance like fools for countless days.

Sun-Drenched Canopy

Under a roof of leaves that gleam,
A silly monkey starts to scheme,
Dropping bananas, oh what a sight,
As we dodge the fruit in sheer delight.

The sun's a jokester, warms our backs,
While ants conspire in tiny packs,
"What's for lunch?" I hear one boast,
"Hope it's not a foot!" they whisper, almost.

The bees buzz in tune with our dance,
As flowers sway, they join in advance,
With every laugh, the light reflects,
In a sun-drenched canopy, joy connects.

We play hide and seek with shadows tall,
While lizards audition for a great fall,
In giggles and grins, life's a playful spree,
In this sunny world, how funny it can be!

Patterns of the Gale

The breeze has a rhythm, quite like a dance,
Bamboo sways to its silly prance.
Parrots squawk jokes like comedians do,
While monkeys throw coconuts just for a view.

Turtles wear sunglasses, looking quite cool,
Sipping on smoothies, they'll make you a fool.
The lizards are gossiping, tails all a-whirl,
As the crabs play charades, their claws in a twirl.

Rain's coming in but don't you fret,
Puddles tomorrow will be a great pet.
We'll splash in the mud, our laughter a song,
Wearing our flip-flops, we'll dance all day long.

So raise up your coconuts, cheer for the gale,
Join in the fun, we'll never grow stale.
In this jungle, where humor is key,
We're the kings and queens of this leafy spree!

Secrets in the Canopy

Up in the trees where the squirrels conspire,
They plot silly pranks and never retire.
A toucan's the judge, with a beak full of sass,
He rules on the shenanigans, all in good class.

The vines twist around like they're telling a tale,
Of raccoons in pajamas, who sneak out at scale.
They raid the fruit stands, giggling with glee,
Swapping out mangoes for peanuts with tea.

Hidden away in a leaf-laden nook,
An owl helps the wise with their baffling book.
He winks through his glasses, so bright and so round,
Cracking wise jokes that make no real sound.

As sunbeams slice through, like humor divine,
Watch out for the ants, they march in a line.
With all of these secrets that nature unveils,
Who needs a step ladder when laughter prevails!

Journey through the Twilight Grove

In twilight's embrace, the glowworms all shine,
They guide us with giggles and skippy red wine.
A sloth says he's fast—well, fast for a sloth,
We'll race him tomorrow; I'll bet he'll be wroth.

Fireflies buzzing like they know the score,
Dance in the dusk, then ask for encore.
A raccoon reads fortunes in leaves made of gold,
Predicts we'll find snacks, if only we're bold.

The shadows grow longer, the stars start to blink,
Frogs croak their wisdom, we stop for a drink.
"Why did the chicken cross?" one frog starts to jest,
"Because it found a discount on twinkly best-dressed!"

The twilight transforms this grove to a stage,
Where every critter stars, releasing their rage.
So let's spin a tale 'neath the vast, twinkling sky,
In a place where the laughs like the fireflies fly!

Beneath the Starlit Veil

Beneath glittering skies, with stars all aglow,
We whisper sweet secrets to breezes below.
A crab in a tuxedo serves snacks on a plate,
With jokes that will tickle, we can hardly wait.

The night air is filled with a giggling sound,
As owls crack wise, their wisdom profound.
"Why don't we ever tell secrets of trees?"
"Because they'd just leaf us; they're bound to the breeze!"

The moon's playing tricks, like a jester at court,
She hides in the clouds, looking for a report.
A raccoon with sweet teeth gives laughter a twist,
Searching for desserts, not a pie he's missed.

So let's raise our cups to the night's merry crew,
With laughter and joy, and a bit of sweet dew.
In this starlit retreat, where giggles prevail,
We dance to the rhythm, beneath the bright veil!

Journey to the Emerald Isles

Pack your bags and bring some snacks,
The sun is shining, no time to relax.
We'll ride a wave on a flamingo float,
Sipping smoothies while we gloat.

The parrot squawks a tune, oh dear,
A beach ball flies, let's persevere!
The sand so warm, it tickles the toes,
But watch out for those crabs with their pose!

A dance-off starts by the sea,
With jellyfish joining, can you see?
We'll do the conga, we'll laugh till we drop,
While the sun is setting, let's never stop!

On emerald shores, we'll sing out loud,
With seagulls dancing, we feel so proud.
This journey's a riot, so don't be shy,
Let's chase some rainbows across the sky!

Rhythm of the Tropical Night

When night falls down, the stars come alive,
The fireflies twinkle, it's time to dive.
We'll dance with the owls, and let out a cheer,
As monkeys start jiving, drawing near.

The drummer's beat is loud and clear,
As boisterous frogs join in the cheer.
A conga line forms, all shades and hues,
Even the sloths find their groove and move!

The moon's got moves, it's winking bright,
Can you believe it? What a sight!
We'll howl like coyotes on this big night spree,
Pretending we're stars – just you and me!

So come take a chance, feel the music and sway,
While under the palms, let's dance away.
With laughter and joy, we'll sing our song,
In the rhythm of night, we truly belong!

Heartbeat of Lush Landscapes

In the jungle, a hiccup, oh what could it be?
A monkey in quest of his lost green pea!
The trees are giggling, the bushes are swaying,
As nature joins in on this wild display.

A parakeet sneezes, paints the air bright,
The flowers are blushing, what a funny sight!
The frogs wear tuxedos for their dance so grand,
While the iguanas make quite the band.

The rush of the river sings sweetly along,
The toucans chime in with a jolly song.
While butterflies hover, chasing each other,
The essence of joy is like no other!

With every heartbeat, the laughter grows loud,
In lush landscapes, it feels like a crowd.
So let's twirl through the ferns, hop over the stream,
In this funny jungle life, we'll live the dream!

In the Shade of Coconut Trees

Under the palms, we lay in the shade,
A tourist lost, just found lemonade.
The coconuts giggle, they tumble and roll,
While crabs throw a dance, it's their main goal.

We've got a sunburn, our noses are red,
With islander hats on, we laugh instead.
A breeze comes by, our snacks take flight,
The birds swoop down, what a silly sight!

The sandcastles crumble in swirls of delight,
As kids chase their dreams, with pure delight.
The ocean waves crash, one splash at a time,
We'll swim with the fish, 'tis a funny rhyme!

So join us beneath where coconuts sway,
We'll pickle our worries, then toss them away.
With joy overflowing, and surfaces gleam,
In the shade of our laughter, we live the dream!

Radiance of Forgotten Shores

On sands of gold, I tripped my way,
Got up to laugh, the seashells sway,
A crab relentless takes off my shoe,
I chase it down, it's faster than you!

The sun's a traitor, burns like a torch,
I found some shade beneath a porch,
My drink's umbrella flies like a kite,
"It's a coconut!" I shout in delight.

A parrot squawks with gossip to share,
"Your hat's gone rogue, it's up in the air!"
I wave and grin, in the salty breeze,
While sunburned folks are doing the freeze.

A seagull swoops low, it's a thief on high,
Snatched my sandwich, oh me, oh my!
Laughing out loud as I barter with fate,
"Two chips for a fry, is that a fair state?"

Chasing the Setting Sun

On golden shores, I made a dash,
To catch the sunset, oh what a clash,
But tripped on a turtle, oh what a sight,
It rolled away, my evening delight!

The sky is painted, orange and red,
While I'm tangled up in my beach bed,
"Is this a sunset, or am I on fire?"
I laugh and roll, my heart lifts higher.

With flip-flops flying, I'm winging it fast,
My drink spills over, man, did it last?
Chasing the clouds like a hungry dog,
"A sunset feast!" I mock from the fog.

This evening's winner is my sunburned face,
The seagulls squawk "You got no grace!"
Yet I embrace the beach's sweet fun,
With laughter echoing under the sun.

Lure of the Hidden Isle

An island whispers secrets untold,
As I set sail, bold and uncontrolled,
But what's that splash? A dolphin grins,
"Welcome aboard!" It laughs and spins.

A treasure map? Now that's a treat,
With 'X' marked down where pirates meet,
But half the clues are written in cheese,
A gouda reward? Oh, with such ease!

Palm trees dance with a clueless sway,
While I try to find the right way,
On hidden shores, all rules are loose,
"Is this a beach or a chicken's truce?"

To the horizon, let my dreams fly,
With a sunburned back and a joyful sigh,
In this jest-filled paradise, let me reside,
With laughter's echo, my faithful guide.

Whispers of the Sea Breeze

When morning breaks with a giggle and cheer,
The ocean chuckles, "Come over here!"
I stumble out, with my morning grind,
A wayward wave steals my breakfast, oh blind!

The breeze carries tales from far and near,
Of sunburned tourists and last night's beer,
I sip my drink, it turns into foam,
A pineapple hat? Guess I'm at home!

Each wave a tale, each tide a jest,
An anchor's my friend, on this wild quest,
With laughter as currency, I trade all day,
For sea-breeze whispers that dance and sway.

So let's toast to shores that never get old,
Where folly shines brighter than any gold,
With winks from the gulls and tales from the sea,
I find my own joy, come laugh with me!

Tides of Enchantment

When the sun dips low, I dance with glee,
A crab steals my flip-flop, oh that's not for me.
Palm trees sway like they're at a show,
Seagulls auditioning for a Broadway glow.

Beach towels spread, a colorful sight,
In the sand, I've lost my snack—oh, what a plight!
Laughter echoes with waves in a race,
Sunburned noses wearing a silly face.

Buckets and spades, a child's delight,
I build a tall castle that's quite a sight.
Complete with a moat that runs dry in the sun,
My kingdom is shaky, but oh, it's such fun!

As the tide rolls in, I wave my last cheer,
Bidding farewell to the laughter and beer.
Tomorrow awaits with more games and sun's light,
In this ocean of joy, everything feels right.

Whispers of the Coastal Winds

The breezy reports bring tales anew,
Of a fish that claims it can dance for a brew.
Shells tell secrets, with giggles inside,
As I chase a sand dollar, it starts to hide.

Hats fly away, a comical sight,
My friend caught one, oh what strange flight!
Bikini tops flapping like flags in the breeze,
In this carnival chaos, we laugh as we please.

The sun spills laughter on the soft shoreline,
Sand between toes, everything feels fine.
With ice creams that topple from cones that are stacked,
We devour delights, making taste buds act.

When dusk paints the skies in a zany hue,
We'll dance with the crickets in flip-flops too.
In the glow of the light, with stars up above,
We'll cap off the night with giggles and love.

Beneath the Mango Canopy

Under mango trees with leaves so wide,
I spot a squirrel taking a fruit-filled ride.
With laughter erupting from each little sound,
   A sticky adventure is waiting around.

Juicy mangoes hanging, a delicious trap,
I reach for a taste, but I slip with a flap.
The juice runs like rivers, so sweet and divine,
Now I'm a fruit ninja on summer's coastline.

Ants hold a party underfoot, oh my!
They're planning a feast when I thought they would fly.
While I munch on snacks with a giggle and cheer,
They're eyeing my sandwich; oh no, disappear!

As sunset descends, we toast to the day,
By sipping on nectar—let's laugh and play.
With the stars joining in on our magical spree,
   This tropical life is wild and carefree.

Escapade in a Sun-Dappled Haven

In a sun-dappled cove, adventure's in sight,
Where sunscreen's a must, and laughter's polite.
With beach balls that bounce high into the air,
I dodge a stray frisbee—oh dear, beware!

Dancing with shadows, we mimic the waves,
Strutting our stuff like silly sea braves.
Collecting shells, each one a prized gem,
While our witty remarks are held in a hem.

The coconut palms speak secrets untold,
As I sip from a coconut that's icy and bold.
My friends make a splash, all perfectly timed,
In this light-hearted whirl, we're perfectly primed.

As twilight descends on this dance of delight,
We gather up stories from day into night.
In this sun-kissed escape, with glee we'll proclaim,
Life's just a beach—let's enjoy all the same!

Serenade of the Paradise Birds

In the jungle, birds don't sing,
They just chat and gossip, it's a funny thing.
With feathers bright and beaks that squawk,
They argue over who's the best at talk.

A parrot claims to know the news,
While toucans argue over different views.
The macaws all act like they're the stars,
As they squabble 'neath the laughing guitars.

Monkeys swing while cracking jokes,
While sloths just hang without any hoax.
The whole jungle bursts with laughter and cheer,
While the sun shines bright like it ain't got a fear.

Oh, the fruit is ripe and the fun's in the air,
With each silly dance and colorful flair.
In paradise, where smiles never fade,
Funny tales, in the wild parade.

Starlit Nights Over Still Waters

Under the stars, the fish seem to giggle,
Making bubbles that burst with a wiggle.
They splash about, with swishes and sways,
Dancing on water in comical ways.

A turtle complains of the weight on his shell,
While frogs croak out notes that are rather swell.
The crickets join in with a quirky trill,
In this nighttime symphony, laughter will spill.

Fireflies blink like they're in a race,
The slowest one wins with a wink of his face.
As the moonlight spills on the rippling lake,
Everyone chuckles for the fun of it's sake.

When morning comes, and the sun peeks through,
The giggles of night fade into the blue.
But the echoes remain in the heart's gentle sway,
As memories twinkle, like stars in the play.

Laughter in the Breeze

In the palm trees, the coconuts chat,
Bouncing laughter like a playful cat.
The wind carries tales of the day's great spree,
Joking with clouds, oh woe is me!

A child climbs high, the branches sway,
With a bird on his shoulder, they wiggle and play.
Together they spin, create a big fuss,
While the sun giggles, minimizing the rush.

Squirrels dance in their crazy attire,
While lizards lounge, hoping to inspire.
Every rustle, every leaf's gentle tease,
Brings forth a chuckle carried by the breeze.

When evening comes, and shadows grow long,
The whole world joins in with a silly song.
For here in the warmth, where smiles set free,
Laughter takes flight like a hummingbee.

Mirage of a Distant Horizon

On the shore, where sands shift and sway,
Waves whisper jokes as they play all day.
Seagulls squawk tales of a fish that got away,
As clams roll their eyes at the salty ballet.

A crab tiptoes in a comical stride,
While a starfish wishes it could glide.
The sun grins down, a big golden tease,
With ticklish rays that dance through the trees.

In the distance, a mirage takes shape,
A beach party promised, like an old drape.
But when you arrive, it's just your own shade,
And laughter erupts as the sun starts to fade.

With evening's glow and a soft cooling breeze,
The shore will echo with fun memories.
So let's not chase what may never be true,
When laughter's the best thing to stick like glue.

Footprints in the Sand

Sandcastles rise, then fall with the tide,
Seagulls laughing, they take to the sky.
A flip-flop flops as I run from the waves,
With every splash, I squeal and I dive.

Sunburned nose, and toes all buried,
Ice cream melting, oh, it's so scary.
We flip a coin to decide who will swim,
But both of us know it's a joint little whim.

Crabs scuttle sideways, they tease and they taunt,
I chase them around in my sun hat gaunt.
With every step, I leave my bright print,
But this sandy song makes my worries hint.

The beach ball bounces, we scramble for goal,
A dance of laughter, nothing's too droll.
With sunshines beaming and smiles so grand,
Here at the shore, let our joys expand.

Tides of Endless Adventure

The waves come crashing, a playful embrace,
Paddling out, I challenge the race.
But oh! The surfboard slips, oh what a sight,
Splash! There it goes, I'm out of my fight.

With each rolling wave, we giggle and shout,
Chasing the foamy white trails about.
My buddy's sunscreen turned him quite glow,
With every new splash, we're putting on a show.

We'll build a raft from some branches we find,
But driftwood's plans are a tad undermined.
The magic boat sinks beneath our own weight,
But we keep on laughing, let's not tempt fate!

So here's to our tales on this sun-soaked spree,
As the sunset paints colors, just you and me.
Every splash tells a story, let's raise a cheer,
For adventure awaits, the horizon is near!

Rituals of the Driftwood

Driftwood dancing, a merry old time,
We craft little boats, oh what a climb!
With twine and some dreams, we make quite a show,
As they bob on the waves, to where? We don't know.

The sea tells us secrets, so wild and so bright,
Like which fish to catch in the shining moonlight.
But instead, let us fish for our hearts' little dreams,
A treasure of laughter, not all as it seems.

Burying treasure? Who needs a map?
When half of it's buried beneath the sand flap.
A Tiki torch joins our rather odd quest,
And our dance with the crabs is a true seaside fest.

So here in the shallows, we learn to let go,
While driftwood glimmers in that golden glow.
Each ritual echoed in giggles so sweet,
In the embrace of the sand, life's complete!

Embrace of the Ocean's Kiss

The ocean waves whisper, "Come and join in,"
Where laughter and splashes make everything spin.
With sand on my feet and a drink in my hand,
The sun's all around, I've a life that's so grand.

Flip-flops abandoned; we dance barefoot on sand,
A conga line forms as my best friend takes a stand.
Shells become trumpets, as seashells do play,
We march to the rhythm, letting worries sway.

Tanned but a bit too much, oh dear me,
Like a lobster turned bright, where's my sunscreen spree?
With giggles and sunburns, we dance with delight,
As the stars peek out, signaling the night.

So here's to the ocean, with kisses so sweet,
In salty embraces, our laughter's complete.
With waves at our backs and dreams in our eyes,
This ocean party is our great surprise!

Fruits of the Dreamers' Realm

In gardens lush, where laughter grows,
The mangoes wear their sunny clothes.
Coconuts dance under the sun,
A party where the fun's never done.

Pineapples joke about their spines,
While bananas slip in goofy lines.
Passion fruits spill, with a wink,
As dreamers munch and sip their drink.

Papayas plot a comedy show,
While guavas giggle down below.
Every fruit has a tale to share,
In the realm of dreams, there's joy to spare.

So join the feast, let your heart roam,
In the land of flavors, you'll feel at home.
Life's a joke, with sweetness to taste,
In the dreamers' realm, there's no time to waste.

Gardens of the Celestial Moon

Under the gaze of the giggling stars,
The moon plants gardens, with lots of jars.
Up in the night, where light is a tease,
Flowers tell jokes on the lightest breeze.

The daisies chuckle in dresses of white,
While violets wink, saying, 'Aren't we bright?'
A tomato moonwalks, feeling so spry,
While cucumbers ponder just how to fly.

Beneath the glow, the herbs have a ball,
Chatting and dancing, they're having a ball.
In this celestial garden, laughter is loud,
Every petal proud, like a happy crowd.

So twirl with the blooms, share in the laze,
In the moon's warm embrace, we'll dance for days.
The garden of whimsy, our laughter a tune,
In the delightful glow of the celestial moon.

Gentle Murmurs of the Rain

Raindrops tap, like a playful song,
Whispering secrets as they dance along.
Puddles giggle, splashing with glee,
The world becomes a stage for spree.

Clouds wear funny hats, fluffy and bold,
While down below, the flowers unfold.
They sway to the rhythm, a cheerful tune,
In the gentle rain, we all feel in bloom.

A dandelion sneezes, 'achoo!' it shouts,
While the tall grass chuckles, shaking about.
The trees sway their branches, having a blast,
In the murmurs of rain, we forget the past.

So join in the fun, let worries shed,
Dance in the droplets, let joy spread.
For in the gentle rains, laughter stays,
A playful ballet that brightens our days.

Painted Skies of Dawn

At dawn, the sky puts on a show,
With colors that dance, all in a row.
The sun yawns wide, stretching so bright,
While clouds giggle, painting the light.

Orange and pink, a vibrant splash,
As daybreak whispers with a hearty laugh.
Birds chirp, 'Rise up! It's time to play!'
In painted skies, we greet the day.

The sun tickles the trees as it climbs,
While squirrels chatter, sharing some rhymes.
Nature's audience, all clapping along,
In the masterpiece where we all belong.

So lift your eyes, let your spirit soar,
In the art of dawn, we can't help but adore.
With painted skies and laughter's embrace,
Every new day is a joyful race.

Waves of Paradise

The ocean calls in sunny glee,
Pineapples surf while coconuts flee.
Flip-flops flying off in a spree,
Laughing crabs dance like they're free.

Seagulls squawk, they steal my fries,
While I sunbathe, they plot their lies.
A beach ball winks with glimmering eyes,
And palm trees sway to my surprise.

Bikinis squeak, the sunscreen sprays,
A fishy friend in a frilly praise.
Sandcastles melting in lazy rays,
While jellyfish wear silly toupee trays.

The tide rolls in with a cheerful grin,
As I'm buried deep in sand, akin.
A coconut falls, I'm hit on the chin,
In this merry land, let the fun begin!

Lush Secrets of the Isles

In a hammock strung, I take my rest,
A monkey steals my snack—it's the best!
Bananas fly with a little jest,
Nature's jokes put patience to the test.

Tall palms whisper silly tunes,
While iguanas groove beneath the moons.
Mangoes tumble down like cartoon loons,
And coconuts chuckle in funny cartoons.

Colorful fish in a parade so grand,
Playing tag with a hat made of sand.
Though my boat wobbles, I still stand,
Finding riches in this crazy land.

When night falls, the fireflies glow,
Light up the giggles, like stars that flow.
Dance with the waves, let worries go,
For this island life is the ultimate show!

Vibrant Horizons

A sunset spills like spilled wine,
With crabs in suits, they sip and dine.
Palms wear sunglasses, looking divine,
As parrots laugh at my cheesy line.

The skies explode in candy hues,
A pig on a surfboard, it surely amuses.
I join the fiesta, in flip-flop shoes,
While the ocean sings its bubbly blues.

A limbo contest under the stars,
With clumsy dancers and massive jars.
Turtles moonwalk, like rock star czars,
Cheers erupt amidst playful scars.

As night embraces the silly crew,
We sing off-key and drink coconut brew.
In this kooky place where laughter grew,
Every horizon shines with something new!

Swaying Rhythm of the Breeze

The breeze whispers secrets, cheeky and bright,
As palm leaves sway to the moon's light.
Sandy toes dance with sheer delight,
While fish in bowties put up a fight.

Flip-flop races take off at dawn,
As seabirds cackle, "Come on, come on!"
With spunky seashells that brag and yawn,
While I attempt to not draw a fawn.

Tanned tourists juggle sunblock tubes,
While snorkeling gear forms quirky cubes.
Crab competitions break all our rube drubs,
As they groove along with our silly jibes.

With laughter ringing in the salty air,
We toast to friendship, without a care.
In this goofy paradise, nothing's rare,
As we feast on warmth, soul, and flair!

Tropical Tides

On sandy shores where coconuts fall,
I tripped on a crab, oh what a call!
With flip-flops flying and laughter in air,
Even the seagulls gave me a stare.

The waves did a dance, a splash and a play,
A fish whispered secrets, but swim away!
I tried to catch sunlight in my palm,
Instead, I just caught a wave that was calm.

Grumpy old turtles, they so ponder,
Why humans wear shorts that are too much of a wonder?
With piña coladas, oh what a fit,
We'll laugh at the waves as they nudge, they won't quit!

But as sunset arrived, the stars came to jest,
They twinkled and winked, giving nature its best.
So let's toast to the night with giggles and cheers,
For fun in the sun washes away all our fears.

Laughter in the Lagoon

In a lagoon where the paddlers glide,
I saw a frog with a sunburned hide.
He croaked such jokes, we all had to laugh,
His punchline slipped, he fell in the bath!

With turtles that race, it's a grand ol' scene,
One in a hat, acting like a marine.
Jumping and splashing, the fish take the bait,
For dinner, a party, let's celebrate fate!

A parrot flew in, with colors so bright,
He squawked out secrets, he could not take flight.
So many bananas, they slipped on the floor,
We laughed as they slipped, what a hullabaloo score!

Let's dance with the crabs, let's sing with the breeze,
Wiggly trees sway, like they're doing the Macaree!
Here in the laughter, let joy be unconfined,
For life's a lagoon where fun is defined.

Sunlit Escapade

Upon a bright beach, so sunny and fair,
I donned my sunglasses, no worries, no care.
But a seagull swooped down, oh what a surprise!
He stole my sandwich right before my eyes!

With waves like a blanket, the sun kissed my nose,
The sand stuck to me, from my feet to my clothes.
I built a sandcastle, so grand, oh so tall,
But a wave came crashing, I guess it was my fall!

Palm trees were swaying, they looked quite absurd,
One dropped a coconut, now that's just plain weird.
I laughed at the mess, and embraced the day,
For funny adventures are just here to stay.

So raise up your glasses to the skies above,
Where laughter and sun are the things that we love.
With a wink to the ocean, let's dance while we may,
In this sunny escapade, we'll find a new way.

Blossoms of the Rainforest

In the rainforest thick, where the monkeys all swing,
One lost his hat, now that's quite the king!
He scratched his head, doing a jig on a vine,
While vines tried to tickle him, everything's fine!

Bright blossoms giggled, with colors so loud,
While frogs serenaded, forming a crowd.
They croaked silly songs, in harmony's tune,
Reminding us all, that life's one big boon!

A sloth took his time, as he climbed up a tree,
He chuckled aloud, dragging all for tea.
With biscuits in hand, he'd slowly confess,
That living like this is nature's best dress!

So dance with the flowers, and join in the fun,
In the heart of the woods, where laughter's not done.
Each petal, each branch, it's a whimsical race,
For in this green wonder, we all find our place.

Floating on a Sea of Serenity

There once was a boat made of cheese,
It floated on waves with the greatest of ease.
But seagulls would swoop,
And they'd steal my soup,
While I laughed as I paddled, feeling the breeze.

With sunscreen applied and a hat slightly askew,
I tried to look cool, but I slipped in the goo.
The fish had a smirk,
As I did my work,
And waved to my friends from my watery view.

Crab cakes danced south while I anchored for lunch,
A dolphin suggested I join in the fun,
But I wore my red shades,
And ignored their charades,
And munched on my sandwich—oh, what a crunch!

As I drifted away on my cheesy delight,
I wondered if seagulls would gift me a kite.
With laughter and cheer,
The ocean was clear,
In my floating domain, everything felt just right.

Journey through Blossoming Trails

On a trek through a jungle, I lost my way,
With vines on my ankles, I shouted, 'Hooray!'
While squirrels just stared,
And raccoons all dared,
To judge my poor fashion, oh what a display!

I tripped on a flower, it bloomed in surprise,
It said, "Do you mind? I have dreams to realize!"
But I couldn't agree,
I was stuck in this tree,
With bees buzzing loudly and darting like spies.

A parrot flew by, with a hat that was neat,
It squawked, "What a nerd! You've got mud on your feet!"
With laughter I grinned,
And joined in the trend,
Dancing with birds to a tropical beat.

Through blossoms and laughter, my spirit was free,
As I twirled with the flora, just me and the bee.
For in nature's embrace,
With mud on my face,
Life's journeys are best with a splash of quirky glee!

Colors of the Endless Summer

In a land where the sun played peek-a-boo,
I thought I was gold, but I looked more like goo.
With sunscreen in blobs,
And flip-flops like mobs,
I danced on the beach as a human fondue.

The sand was so warm, it gave me a cheer,
While the waves tickled toes and called me near.
But each splash and each dive,
Made the seagulls contrive,
To drop their own snacks like they owned the sphere.

I painted my nails in a riot of hues,
While the bugs took my chips for their own little snooze.
They partied all night,
Inviting the light,
And I joined in the fun with no time to refuse.

So here's to the chaos, the colors, and more—
Where laughter erupts as you dance on the shore.
With each goofy twirl,
And sand in a whirl,
The endless delights keep my spirit to soar.

Echoes of an Ocean Breeze

There's a whispering breeze that's quite charming,
It nudged me awake and kept me from harm-ing.
With sand in my hair,
And jellyfish flair,
I giggled and flailed while the waves kept disarming.

A crab with a bow tie approached me with flair,
It asked for a dance without any despair.
But my moves were a mess,
I'll surely confess,
I tripped on my towel, not light as a air!

As I lounged on my towel, feeling quite sly,
A squirrel with sunglasses winked at the sky.
It brought me a drink,
With a mischievous wink,
And said, "Here's a refreshment; don't even ask why!"

With echoes of laughter and waves in control,
I embraced the humor that brightened my soul.
In this beachy retreat,
Where the goofy can meet,
Life's whimsical charms make us all feel whole.

A Symphony of Warm Breezes

A parrot sings a silly tune,
While monkeys dance beneath the moon.
Bananas slip, a comical sight,
As palm trees sway, oh what delight!

The sun is bright, no hats in sight,
Or folks will leave their heads in fright.
Warm breezes tickle noses red,
And flip-flops fly, as laughter spreads!

Coconuts drop with gentle thuds,
Creating comedies in the buds.
The beach is full of joyful cheer,
As tourists trip and let out a squeal!

Bikinis dance like fish on land,
While sunscreen's found in grains of sand.
A symphony of giggles rise,
In paradise beneath blue skies!

Secrets of the Coral Reef

A fish in a tux jumps with flair,
While clowns in the ocean drop their hair.
Seahorses tease the passing brine,
As turtles giggle and sip on wine.

Corals arrange a playful show,
With starfish posing in their glow.
The crabs pull pranks, they scurry and weave,
While octopuses weave up their sleeves!

A pufferfish blows up with pride,
A balloon at the ocean's side.
Jellyfish jiggle, swaying with grace,
In this underwater, funny place!

Secrets bubble in tides of joy,
Even the barnacles start to annoy.
The ocean floor is filled with glee,
Where laughter echoes eternally!

Colors of a Balmy Sky

Clouds of cotton candy dance,
Balloons float by in a silly trance.
Sunshine drizzles like melted gold,
While the sunsets shine in colors bold.

Fluffy pillows in motion fly,
Kites soar up high in the blue sky.
The wind is friendly, it tickles the trees,
As laughter floats along with the breeze.

Splashing in puddles, oh what fun,
Chasing rainbows just to run.
Colors burst like laughter's sound,
In this joyful world where glee is found!

With every hue, a smile ignites,
Chasing the clouds, both day and night.
The balmy sky, a canvas bright,
Keeps spirits dancing in delight!

Echoes of the Gentle Tide

Waves whisper secrets to the shore,
While shells giggle, begging for more.
The tide rolls in with a playful swish,
Launching crabs toward their ocean wish.

Flip-flops fly, like fish in flight,
As seagulls dive, oh what a sight!
Each splash of water's a sight to see,
Like a shower of giggles, wild and free.

The sun dips low, a comedy feast,
As shadows stretch, the laughter's released.
Stars peek out with a wink and a nod,
While sandcastles face the ocean's prod.

Echoes of laughter ride the tide,
Filling the air with all kinds of pride.
In this world where humor abide,
Every wave brings joy, side by side!

Paradise in Every Grain of Sand

Grains of sand slip through your toes,
Each one whispers where the sun glows.
A crab scuttles by, so bold and spry,
Wondering why humans just lie and sigh.

Palm trees sway, they dance with flair,
While I just try to brush off my hair.
Seagulls cackle; they think they're grand,
As I build castles that quickly disband.

My sunscreen's a mess, a slippery lotion,
I might as well swim in a giant ocean.
Flip-flops flying, a true fashion crime,
I forgot my towel—oh, what a time!

But laughter is golden, a sun's warm embrace,
In this sandy kingdom, I find my place.
With each wave that crashes, a joyous cheer,
Life's a beach, and paradise is near!

The Lure of Coastal Dreams

A hammock sways between two trees,
I knock my drink, oh, what a tease!
The parrot squawks, 'You call that style?'
As I try to relax for a little while.

Shells in pockets, a curious find,
The seagulls steal what's left behind.
While tossing seaweed, I have to grin,
How can this chaos not be a win?

The surfboard acts like my long-lost friend,
But it flips me over; oh, what a trend!
Sand in my sandwich, crunchy delight,
Did I just eat that? Well, that's alright!

As evening falls, the fireflies gleam,
I dream of cupcakes, a sugary dream.
In this coastal haven, life's a charade,
Who knew fun could be this well-made?

Reverie of the Mangrove's Heart

Mangroves sway in a muddled dance,
As I trip and splash, oh what a chance!
A lizard laughs, 'You call that a stroll?'
While I search for treasure, that slippery shoal.

The mud is squishy, a sticky embrace,
As my friends all giggle, they know my face.
I try to blend in with the flora and vine,
But the bugs find me first—it's almost divine!

Crabs in a meeting, they plot and they scheme,
While I'm stuck here, caught in a dream.
Paddling slowly, I make my way,
Too bad I forgot my sunscreen today!

But who cares? This mischief is real,
In this tangled love, my heart begins to heal.
With laughter echoing under the sun,
I declare mangroves my favorite fun!

Where the Ocean Meets the Sun

Waves crash down, a slippery show,
I try to surf, but my balance won't grow.
The sunbeams chuckle, they wink and tease,
As I face-plant in foam, 'Oh, what a breeze!'

Children's laughter, like music it sings,
While sand gets tangled in all of my things.
A seagull swoops down, eyeing my fries,
As I hide my sandwich beneath cloudy skies.

The sunset spills colors, a painter's delight,
But I'm caught in sand, with no end in sight.
The tide comes calling, a cheeky request,
As I hold my shoes, trying to rest.

Yet joy fills the air, my spirit ignites,
With the ocean's embrace, oh, what a night!
In this watery world, I find my pace,
Where laughter greets waves in a warm embrace.

Oasis of Heartfelt Whispers

In a beach chair's embrace, I recline,
While seagulls dance on the edge of the brine.
My sunscreen's gone rogue, oh what a sight,
As I look like a lobster, a pure fright!

Coconuts fall with a thud and a crash,
I rush to dodge them, oh no! What a splash!
The palm trees giggle, my mischief they see,
As I slip on my flip-flops, daredevil of glee!

A hammock sways low, inviting my fate,
But my snack starts to vanish, oh mate, what a state!
A squirrel in shades snatches my chips,
And I watch as my lunch goes on daring trips!

But laughter erupts with each silly blunder,
As the waves serenade, I toss away wonder.
In this blissful chaos, my heart finds its cheer,
In this whispering oasis, there's nothing to fear!

The Call of Adventure

Pack up your worries, they can stay home,
With a suitcase of dreams, together we roam.
A map that is torn, and a compass that spins,
We chart out our course where the fun always begins!

At the beach, I declare, the rules bend and sway,
Building castles of sand, I'm the king for the day.
But the tide comes with fury, it sweeps them away,
I shout like a pirate, 'Arrgh, come what may!'

A parrot named Polly squawks proud and so loud,
She narrates my saga to a curious crowd.
With planks on my feet, I plunge into surf,
Then slip and slide, like I'm being rebirthed!

Oh the stories we'll tell in our foolish delight,
Adventures await in the stars shining bright.
With laughter and smiles, we'll conquer the sea,
This call of fun, oh, it's meant just for me!

Flowing with Nature's Pulse

Under the sun, where the bananas grow,
My dance moves are wild, a true tropical show!
The river quips softly, with gurgles and laughs,
As I jump in the water, make silly splashes!

The monkeys are clapping, they mimic my spin,
With a bunch of ripe fruits, they invite me in.
I join in their frolic, hilarity reigns,
As we swing from the branches, ignoring our chains!

A turtle named Larry, with style so slick,
Taught me to glide and take life as a trick.
But I tripped on a root, oh what a sight!
The forest erupted with laughter that night!

To flow with this nature, it's a wild ride,
With giggles aplenty, and friends by my side.
In this vibrant jungle, where joy keeps on pulsing,
Life dances around, laughter always repulsing!

Rhapsody of the Emerald Waters

Emerald waves bounce with a whimsical cheer,
I dive in headfirst, because I have no fear.
A fish grins at me, with a wink and a flip,
We share this great party, I'm ready to dip!

Mermaids with tambourines swirl among corals,
They sing me sweet sonnets, under the spirals.
But a shellfish named Chuck tells a hilarious joke,
And I choke on the saltwater—oh what a poke!

With every wild splash, a joke seems to bloom,
My snorkel's a cannon, bubbling fun in the room.
The seaweed, my dance partner, sways as I sway,
We're lost in this rhapsody, come join the fray!

So here's to the waters, both deep and so bright,
Where laughter abounds, and the stars shine at night.
In this joyful embrace, we'll cherish the tide,
As the sea whispers secrets, with joy as our guide!

Island Whispers

In a hammock swaying low,
Banana peels fly to and fro.
Coconuts chuckle up high,
As tourists trip and ask why.

Pelicans borrow my sunscreen,
Chasing seagulls on the green.
Crabs perform a side-step jive,
While I just try to survive.

Bikini tops in disarray,
Trying to keep the waves at bay.
Laughter echoes through the air,
As I search for my lost hair.

Sipping drinks with tiny straws,
Counting fish and their faux pause.
Every sip a splashy cheer,
In this paradise, I adhere.

Beneath the Canopy's Embrace

Chasing lizards in the shade,
Where the ants have made a raid.
Mangoes drop with a big splat,
Blame it on the sneaky cat.

Laughter rings 'neath leafy green,
Where the branches form a screen.
Mosquitoes dancing in delight,
Taking bites that are just right.

Jungle vines like laughing snakes,
Twisting paths with funny aches.
A toucan chuckles on a branch,
While I attempt a silly dance.

Sunbeams peek through gaps so wide,
While I trip and try to slide.
Swatting bugs with grand finesse,
Forest life's a playful mess.

Dance of the Palm Fronds

Palm trees wiggle to the beat,
As I shuffle with two left feet.
Bananas giggle, start to sway,
Hoping to join the cabaret.

Coconuts line up for fun,
Bouncing in the hot sun.
Dancing shoes, all worn and torn,
Underneath the palms, I'm sworn.

Tiki torches flicker bright,
While the shadows join the fight.
Butterflies with grace do twirl,
As I trip and watch them swirl.

Wet towels round my flamingo,
With a splash and giddy show.
Underneath the moonlit glint,
We all dance—each step, a hint.

Sunlit Shores Calling

Waves that giggle at my toes,
Salty breezes, funny flows.
Shells that whisper countless tales,
Beach balls bouncing, oh the fails!

Sandy sunscreen turns me white,
I become a glimmering sight.
Frisbees flying clean off course,
As laughter echoes with no remorse.

Seagulls squawking overhead,
Stealing snacks, they quickly fled.
Sun hats spinning on the ground,
While I'm busy looking around.

Chasing waves with clammy feet,
This paradise can't be beat.
Giggling as I take a dive,
In this chaos, I feel alive!

Choreography of the Night Sky

The stars are dancing, quite the show,
Twinkling lights in the night, whoa!
A moon in a tutu, spinning with flair,
While comets are laughing, floating in air.

The planets are partners, doing a waltz,
But Venus just stumbled, oh how it faults!
Mars wore a top hat, a sight to behold,
While Jupiter's jokes never seem to get old.

Saturn's rings sparkle like silver bling,
As shooting stars prance; what fun they bring!
Constellations chuckle, each in their place,
Making the heavens a silly embrace.

So join in the giggles, let your heart soar,
The cosmos is laughing, who could ask for more?
In this jestful ballet across the vast night,
Let's dance with the stars till the morning light.

Veils of Mystique

Behind the curtain of leaves so lush,
Lies a squirrel in shades, creating a hush.
With sunglasses on, it poses anew,
Like the king of the jungle, for an evening barbecue!

A turtle in flip-flops, strutting with pride,
While parrots gossip, their colors collide.
Coconuts chuckle, they hang from the trees,
Joking about breezes that tease with a squeeze.

A lizard in sequins, oh so refined,
Sips coconut water, oh how unconfined!
The grasshoppers chirp a melodious tune,
As the fog rolls in, a cheeky raccoon!

So take off your cares, let the laughter ensue,
In a world where the quirky come out to construe.
With nature's surprises that always delight,
Join the veils of mystique, from morning till night.

Fluid Dreams of Distant Shores

Wave upon wave, the ocean sings,
A crab wearing shades, minding its things.
With sandcastles built, just to be washed,
A seagull swoops down, 'I'm not even bothered!'

The dolphins are giggling, leaping in style,
While octopi juggle, it's all worth the while.
Starfish are plotting a dance on the sand,
While clams show off pearls, oh isn't it grand?

The sunset paints skies with colors so bright,
While turtles race home, oh what a sight!
Shells whisper secrets of journeys they've been,
As laughter spills over this joyful marine.

So swim with the tide, let your spirit unwind,
In fluid dreams soft, where joy's intertwined.
The shores are alive, with mirth and delight,
Dance with the waves, till the stars come to light.

Symphony of Life and Laughter

The jungle orchestra wakes with a cheer,
From morning's first light to the end of the year.
With monkeys on drums, and parrots that croon,
It's a riot of sounds that's making you swoon!

A frog on a fiddle plays tunes so sublime,
While a flamingo claps, keeping perfect time.
Trees sway to the music, a gentle parade,
As bees buzz along in a festive charade.

The laughter of children floats through the air,
As they dance through the meadows without a care.
Each note of the symphony, wild and free,
Brings joy to the heart, a sweet jubilee.

So join in the chorus, let your spirit sing,
Feel the rhythm of life that nature will bring.
With moments of laughter, let the joy be rife,
In this beautiful symphony, celebrate life!

Beneath the Golden Sun

Palm trees sway, oh what a sight,
With coconuts dropping left and right.
Sipping drinks, they clink and cheer,
Laughing loud, no worries here.

Crabs doing dances, quite a show,
In their tiny tuxedos, they steal the glow.
Sunburned noses parade on the sand,
As flip-flops fly from a careless hand.

A parrot squawks a cheeky tune,
Hiding treasures 'neath the moon.
Beach balls bouncing, laughter galore,
As the sun dips low, we shout for more.

Under the skies of vibrant hue,
We've got no plans, just me and you.
With every ray and wave that sways,
Life's a game we love to play.

Exotic Echoes

In the jungle, a monkey swings,
Dressed in shades, oh how he blings!
Bananarama's on replay,
As he grooves in his hairy way.

Lizards wear the finest style,
On their backs, they wear a smile.
Chasing each other, what a race,
With quick little feet, they keep the pace.

Tropical frogs in a chorus croak,
Ribbit here and ribbit there, oh what a joke!
They're rehearsing for a big debut,
In a swampy bar, just me and you.

With hips that sway and joy in the air,
Missed my chance, my drink's in a flare!
The jungle's alive, it never sleeps,
Among the laughter, nature peeps.

Serenade of the Stars

At night the stars perform their show,
While the fireflies put on a glow.
Dancing crickets play their band,
In the cool grass, hand in hand.

The moon wearing shades, a sight to see,
Sipping on milk (or was it tea?).
While dolphins leap in the calm bay,
Singing tunes till the break of day.

Tiki torches flicker with glee,
In the warm breeze, just you and me.
We chuckle at the fuss of the day,
In our little paradise, come what may.

So let's twirl beneath the starlit beams,
Lost in laughter and silly dreams.
Under this sky, so vast and free,
Life is fun, come be silly with me!

Haven of Colorful Wings

Butterflies flaunt their outfits bright,
Painting the air, oh what a sight!
They've got moves we can't outshine,
With their flutter, they spin in line.

Bees buzz by, they're quite the crew,
Sweet as honey, they know it's true.
In their garden, they make a fuss,
'Pollinate faster!' they laugh amongst us.

Parrots gossip, oh what a tale,
In vivid colors, they never pale.
They squawk about every silly thing,
In this haven, they wear a ring.

So join the party, don't be shy,
In this vibrant world, we all can fly.
With laughter ringing 'neath the sun,
We find that life is simply fun!

www.ingramcontent.com/pod-product-compliance
Lightning Source LLC
Chambersburg PA
CBHW072131070526
44585CB00016B/1630